MW00781723

HowExpert Presents

Burlesque Dancer 101

A Professional Burlesque Dancer's Quick Guide on How to Learn, Grow, Perform, and Succeed at the Art of Burlesque Dancing From A to Z

HowExpert with Emilie Declaron

For more tips related to this topic, visit HowExpert.com/burlesque.

Recommended Resources

- HowExpert.com – Quick 'How To' Guides on All Topics from A to Z by Everyday Experts.
- HowExpert.com/free – Free HowExpert Email Newsletter.
- HowExpert.com/books – HowExpert Books
- HowExpert.com/courses – HowExpert Courses
- HowExpert.com/clothing – HowExpert Clothing
- HowExpert.com/membership – HowExpert Membership Site
- HowExpert.com/affiliates – HowExpert Affiliate Program
- HowExpert.com/writers – Write About Your #1 Passion/Knowledge/Expertise & Become a HowExpert Author.
- HowExpert.com/resources – Additional HowExpert Recommended Resources
- YouTube.com/HowExpert – Subscribe to HowExpert YouTube.
- Instagram.com/HowExpert – Follow HowExpert on Instagram.
- Facebook.com/HowExpert – Follow HowExpert on Facebook.

Table of Contents

Chapter 5: How to perform in your first show

Introduction

Welcome fellow burlesque enthusiast! Whether you chose this little How to Become a Burlesque Dancer book by curiosity or with a firm desire to become a burlesque starlet, get ready to enter a world beyond anything you've ever known before.

Burlesque as an art form is not new, and it encompasses a multitude of styles, performers, shows and cultural manifestations. For a newcomer, it might be a little daunting to make your way through the mass of information that can be found online or on paper.

Burlesque is different from other artistic and theatrical activity, in that knowing how to and where to start is not as straightforward. If you want to become an actor, you join a theatre class or drama group. If you wish to be a painter, you pick up a paintbrush and start painting, or you take drawing lessons. The same goes for music, sculpture, dance...Burlesque on the other hand, always seems shrouded in mystery for the uninitiated.

Burlesque has kept a bit of its scandalous aura since the 18th century, and I lost count of the amount of times I heard "I would love to try burlesque but I wouldn't dare", "this is beautiful but I wouldn't know how to", and more from audience members after shows.

Truth is, anyone can do burlesque if they're passionate enough about it! And trust me, the more you start learning about it, the more involved and obsessed you will become. Burlesque has this way to pull you in.

So forget the mundane for a moment, forget about the day job, and immerse yourself into a universe where rhinestones are essential, glitter is part of everyday life, and champagne is not only made for drinking.

You will discover incredible performers, become familiar with new idols, learn the tips to make yourself look like a showgirl and the tricks to look fabulous on stage.

This How to book aims to provide you with all the tools you might need to start a burlesque career yourself.

You might be a "newbie" as new performers are called in the industry, or you might have taken a few classes and wonder how to make the jump to become a professional.

Maybe you have always been in the audience until now, wondering if you will one day dare to step on the stage also, or maybe you've already performed at a few shows and wonder how you could improve your burlesque persona and become more successful.

You might even be a "burlesque virgin": you have never been to a real live burlesque show, and you want to know more about this glamorous art form.

Whoever you are, once you've read through this entire book, you will possess all the tools necessary to launch and develop your burlesque career.

Let's start, shall we?

Chapter 1: Venturing in the Burlesque Universe

If you're still rather new, or even completely new to burlesque, you may not be familiar with the origins of the art form, or with its most famous stars from the early days. It's important to learn a bit about the way it all started, especially if you intent to perform professionally.

Type "Burlesque" into any search engine or YouTube, and you will get an array of very diverse results, going from a movie with Christina Aguilera to can-can dancers outfits on EBay, with mentions of Italian theatre and stripper shoes provider thrown in for good measure.

Let's dive into the History of this fascinating world.

Know your Burlesque History

The origins of burlesque

- What is burlesque really, and where did it all start?

A quick research on the Oxford Dictionary will give you two answers: one stating that burlesque is "An absurd or comically exaggerated imitation of something, especially in a literary or dramatic work; a parody"; the other, more recent definition will tell you that burlesque nowadays is "A variety show, typically including striptease"[1].

So how on earth did burlesque go from theatre and literature to stripping onstage?

In the 17th century, burlesque was a theatrical and literary genre in which women often played men parts. This was done to get laughs from the audience, but at the same time it meant the women on stage wore tights that showed the shape of their legs, a rather daring feat for the times! (or oohlala in French...)

Burlesque was brought to America and became an instant hit there. The first burlesque troupe to come to the country was called the British Blondes, who caused an outrage when they showed up in men's clothes – again, showing more legs than was common in those times. Obviously, the scandal meant their show was an instant hit, and soon burlesque was an integral part of American variety shows, with the appeal relying largely on being able to see women wearing less than was acceptable in society.

Scandals and "Hoochie-Coochie"

Whilst England moves towards different types of entertainment in the Edwardian era, burlesque

---

[1] Oxford Dictionary, https://en.oxforddictionaries.com/definition/burlesque, last accessed April 30, 2018.

continued being popular in the US, and slowly started to move towards the form we know today. Comedy acts slowly became purely dancing acts, with more and more revealing clothing.

Meanwhile, in late 19th century France, the Moulin Rouge and the Folies Bergères opened, both showcasing French can-can dancers performing daring kicks and revealing their undergarments.

Burlesque gradually became more risqué and integrated a lot of belly-dancing influences, with suggestive "hoochie-coochie" dances gaining popularity.

The 1930s is hailed as the decade when burlesque became truly innovative, and some stars from the era invented routines that are still used as an inspiration to these days – we will come back to them very shortly!

Then... sadly morality laws and censorship started taking their toll on the business. Burlesque lingered until the late 50s but its heydays were gone... that is, until its incredible revival which started in the 1990s with Dita Von Teese!

Vintage Burlesque Queens: Gipsy Rose Lee

- Let's meet a few of the early burlesque queens who made the art form what it is today. You will soon find out that many of the classic burlesque routines you know and love are actualization from older routines, invented by the pioneers of the style.

- Knowing a few of the veterans of the style will help you choose your own preferred burlesque style and will give you ideas when creating your burlesque stage persona.

- Firstly, it's impossible to talk about classic burlesque stars without mentioning Gypsy Rose Lee.

Gipsy got hired as a burlesque dancer in a small theatre. Legend has it that as she was dancing on stage, her dress strap snapped... and she ended up making the "accident" a part of her routine

Gipsy Rose Lee very quickly became a star, and by the mid 1940s she was the main performer at Minsky's. She was known as the intellectual stripper, she put the "tease" in strip-tease, sometimes barely revealing anything at all! Her most famous routine, "The Psychology of a Stripteaser" can be found easily online, and is a lesson to all budding burlesque dancers in the art of teasing and keeping the audience entertained.

Her stripping style is rarely replicated these days, but she certainly has heiresses in the burlesque world today. Jo Weldon in New York for example has been performing and writing about burlesque since the late 90s and continuing in the same intellectual burlesque vein Gipsy invented.

- Now for our second classic burlesque star. If you've been to burlesque shows or watched any documentary about burlesque, you've certainly seen routines performed with large feather fans. We'll get back to the technique behind this classic intricate dance later, let's focus on its creator.

Sally Rand, the Fan Dance Star

It is rumored that Sally's iconic fan dance, still emulated to these days, started by accident. A young Sally bought very large ostrich fans with the intention to turn them into a dress for an audition later during the day... when it turned out she had no time to do so, she went to the audition wearing the fans only!

Sally performed with a flesh colored outfit that made her appear entirely naked under her fans. Her famous routine was widely copied by other burlesque dancers. In fact, other performers claim to have invented it, but that's a story for another time!

- Fan dances are still a staple of any burlesque performer's routine portfolio nowadays, and it's not the only classic routine Sally Rand invented. She also created a routine that saw her perform into a giant bubble, partly so she could deal with the cold when performing outdoors. She certainly started the love story between burlesque dancers and giant props!

An updated version of this routine can be seen in the classic "balloon pop" often enjoyed by newcomers to the world of burlesque performance. We'll come back to it shortly.

Lili St Cyr's bathtub

Only one classic burlesque star from the 1940s era
became more famous and better paid than Gipsy Rose
Lee, and her stage name was Lili St Cyr.

She was famous for performing in transparent
bathtubs which got her arrested... and inspired
countless modern performers, notably the Queen of
Burlesque Dita Von Teese, who regularly performs in
tubs and man-size martini glasses (a routine
popularized by Venus Delight, another legend).

Bump n' Grind and... Tassel Twirling!

"Hoochie-Coochie", inspired by belly-dancing,
marked a sexier turn in the history of burlesque. Many
claim Little Egypt was the first to bring a belly-
dancing feel to her dancing at the World's Columbian
Exposition in 1893. By the 1950s, Hoochie-Coochie
had become bump and grind, a style still widely
practiced by burlesque dancers over the world today.

Golden Era stars of burlesque bump and grind include
notably Crystal Starr and Tempest Storm, the living
legend who only retired in 2012, age 82!

To conclude our section on classic burlesque stars, I
would like to mention the living legend that is Satan's
Angel, the Devil's Own Mistress, Queen of the Fire
Tassels. Satan's Angel started performing in the
1960s, and quickly became famous on the burlesque
scene for her extravagant stage persona. She invented

a tassel-turning trick rarely emulated since: she would set fire to her nipple tassels and turn energetically until the fire would die out!

The different types of burlesque: find which appeals to you the most and develop your style

Learning a little bit about the different types of burlesque is important, as it will help you decide what you like most, and where you want to take your burlesque persona and your acts. Don't worry if you're not sure yet, your style might change a lot during your career, and that's perfectly fine! You can also decide to switch between styles, have classic routines and more experimental ones, after all burlesque is all about freedom.

Let's have little overview of different styles of burlesque.

The Classic vs Neo debate

- I cannot start this chapter without talking about the core of many debates in the burlesque industry... the infamous "classic burlesque versus neo-burlesque" talk. Ask any burlesque dancer or any burlesque enthusiast about their opinion regarding the difference between classic and neo-burlesque, and you will probably hear a different opinion from every performer!

Diving into the details would require a full book! Commonly however, when people oppose classic /traditional burlesque to neo-burlesque, they will picture classic burlesque as a showgirl affair: all glamour, rhinestones, sequins, feather fans, boas and long gowns; whereas neo-burlesque will be seen as something more avant-garde and might cover anything from comedy burlesque, to art performances or nerdy performances.

Some go as far as saying that neo-burlesque is in fact closer in style to the Golden Age of the art form, and the wit of Gypsy, than to the stripping aspect which came later.

- That said, whether you consider yourself to be a traditional performer or a neo-burlesque performer, there is a wide range of styles you can explore.

Traditional burlesque can encompass: showgirl, vaudeville, comedy... anything that brings the audience back to the golden era or to the 1950s burlesque queens.

If what you love in burlesque is the glamour, the mind-blowing sparkly outfits, if you dream of being a 1940s/1950s movie star, if you have a love of all things vintage and fancies yourself a modern day pin-up... then traditional Showgirl burlesque is made for you.

If you have a love for the Golden Era stars, if you admire the wit of Gipsy Rose Lee, if you want your routine to make the audience laugh, then explore the comedy and vaudeville options.

- Neo-burlesque often adds a layer of current pop culture, gender exploration, and / or performance art.

The 00s saw the birth of nerd burlesque for example, with performers catering to the audience love of sci-fi TV shows and movies – check out the Suicide Girls Blackheart Burlesque Stormtrooper routine for example.

Burlesque offers the possibility for men and women to explore their gender, sensuality and sexuality in ways that wouldn't be possible in other art forms. Take the example of the World Famous Bob, who self-describes as a female-female spiritual transsexual and turns the ideas we have about women and femininity on their head.

I am only grazing the top of the iceberg here, there is almost as many different styles of burlesque as there are performers. You will find your own way. The important thing is that you keep learning about the art form, keep watching videos of vintage performances, keep going to shows to see newcomers and stars of our times, and figure out what works best for you.

Who will you be on stage?

Now we've had a quick overview of the History of Burlesque, you're a bit more familiar with its legends, and you're aware burlesque performances can be traditional and glamorous or daring and revolutionary, or a mix of both, let's dive deeper and consider a few styles that are widely known in the industry. See which appeals to you the most, it will help you deciding what type of routine you would like to be doing.

Cheesecake Burlesque

- Cheesecake is a style of burlesque and, like its name indicates, it relies on acting a bit "cheesy". This is your super cute, winking, falsely innocent girl-next-door burlesque. Influenced by the 1950s pin-up imagery, with wide-eyed beauties "accidentally" revealing a bit too much. Think Bettie Page and her innocent smile even in her sexier shoots, or old pin-up drawings that are still so popular these days. Cheesecake burlesque is very character-driven, it relies a lot on the personality of the performer and on facial expressions. It incorporates a lot of comedy and acting aspects, and does not necessarily rely on the dance moves as much.

Cheesecake burlesque is great if as a beginner you don't have the confidence to go all-out on the sexiness, and feel more comfortable being cute, cheeky and less aggressively sexual. It's also perfect if you feel more like a performer than a dancer.

Cheesecake is also very tongue-in-cheek and funny, sometimes even a bit silly, so if you fancy yourself as much as a stripper as a comedian, it's definitely the one for you. If you want your audience to laugh but also reveal in your sexy side in a cute way, you might want to check out some famous cheesecake routines and see if that might work for you. Anna Fur Laxis is the queen of the genre, check out her Bettie Page routine.

Showgirl

- Showgirl burlesque is a promoter's favorite. This is what most people think of when they hear burlesque. Whereas Cheesecake Burlesque is more character-driven, Showgirl Burlesque is all about the glamour. It's a throwback to the Golden Era and vintage Hollywood stars. Think rhinestones, feathers, vintage hairdos and make-up, elaborate costumes, giant props and champagne bottles.

The most famous performer of the Showgirl style is of course Dita Von Teese, who is famous for performing in huge Martini glasses in bejeweled costumes. Catherine D' Lish, Bettsie Bon Bon, Immodesty Blaize and Sukki Singapora are other famous faces who perform Showgirl Burlesque.

Showgirl Burlesque is for you if you have a love for all things glamorous, if you've always dreamt of being a vintage starlet, if you're more Marilyn Monroe than Bettie Page... Showgirl Burlesque reveals in ultra femininity and implies to have beautifully crafted costumes and props – which is doable on a budget as we will see later.

Neo-burlesque

Neo-burlesque as we saw earlier can mean and encompass many things, but is usually considered as anything not Classic, or some say as any burlesque performed since the revival of the scene.

There are many sub-genres of burlesque that have appeared since the late 1990s: gore-lesque (a horror take on burlesque, with routines often inspired by classic horror movies) or nerd-lesque (nerdy-burlesque with routines inspired by super-heros, fantasy or sci-fi movies, and video-games) for example, as well as many other examples that do not fit in the Classic Showgirl Burlesque category.

The choice of songs is also often different in neo-burlesque. Whereas vintage-inspired performers might often choose vintage songs or classical music, neo-burlesque performers tend to go for songs that are not typically associated with burlesque: rock music, movie soundtrack, everything is permitted!

Comedy

Comedy burlesque puts the emphasis on playing a character and telling a story to the audience. Many classic or neo-burlesque routines have elements of comedy, and cheesecake burlesque is often also funny. Comedy burlesque sometimes involves little stripping and teasing.

Boylesque!

Boylesque is simply burlesque performed by men. There are more women burlesque dancers however, there are more and more men performers, who evolve in an array of different styles. Check out Warren Speed for comedy burlesque, Tom Harlow for old school Hollywood glamour and fetish routines.

So you see, there are many different styles of burlesque you could perform. You don't have to choose now, nor at all if you prefer. You can have various routines in different styles... of course your persona might evolve with time and you might find yourself doing something very different a few months or a few years into your career! Changing and evolving is part of the journey.

Pick a unique name

If your burlesque persona is very well-defined, for example if you intend to perform mostly cheesecake vintage with a 50s vintage feel, or if you have a "gimmick" or specialty, like breathing fire or hula-hooping, then you could find a name that will tell the audience what you're about.

Otherwise, try to find a name that you really like or means something to you, as it's not always easy to rebrand later, once people know you under a certain name.

Burlesque performers who mostly perform classic showgirls business tend to go for vintage style names: Dita Von Teese, Catherine D' Lish, Betsy Rose, Roxy D' Lite; foreign sounding names are also a hit: Michelle L'Amour, Loulou La Duchesse de Riere, Lola Van Ella; alliterations are well liked and easy to remember: Bettsie Bon Bon, Havana Hurricane, Bella Blue; some names are humoristic or play on words: Jett Adore, Jeez Loueez, Carman Havalook, Dirty Martini... The important is that your name is original and unique.

Check that nobody else does burlesque under that name!

Know your audience

- One last note on the different types of burlesque: some styles might work better in particular countries. Comedy and nerd burlesque for example, is becoming extremely popular in the US. In the UK, more and more shows feature daring, original performances, with London Burlesque Festival even having a Twisted Revue dedicated to the wonderful and the bizarre in burlesque. In Eastern Europe, the burlesque comeback is more recent and a lot of the events feature more traditional, showgirl burlesque, or an updated version with less stripping and more dancing (think Burlesque, the movie with Cher and Christina Aguilera). In France, there are many small cabarets that have opened and offer performances as far removed from the Crazy Horse or the Moulin Rouge as you can imagine, with daring, gender-bending, humoristic acts. Check out Le Cabaret Burlesque in Lyon for example.

Knowing your audience will certainly help you decide what acts to put forward when you apply to shows, but don't forget that the essential is to do what you love.

Now we've had a brief overview of various burlesque styles and have an idea of which style you prefer, let's focus on a few classic routines you might want to add to your repertoire. These three routines are certainly traditional, though you can make them your own and update them to your taste.

A Few Traditional Routines

The "Balloon Pop" and how to perform it successfully

- Let's start with a routine particularly loved by newcomers and seasoned performers alike. The Balloon Pop requires very little costume wise: a bag of balloon ready to blow, nipple pasties or tassels, underwear and stockings/heels if you wish.

The principle is simple too: the performer starts with an array of balloons covering their body, then pops the balloon one by one – or sometimes two at a time for added effect, until they are in their underwear or pasties.

The performer may use a needle, a hairpin, a feather, or anything they choose to blow the balloons. One of the most famous current Balloon Pop routine is performed with Dirty Martini, and she blows them with a lit cigarette.

There are many ways to hide your pins (or whatever you want to use to pop your balloons) on stage. Have a look at Vendetta Vain's balloon routine for example, where she dresses as a cowgirl and uses a pin hidden in a fake gun.

Now there are a few things to consider when you want to perform a balloon pop routine:

- The space. Where will you change? This is an important consideration, as in the event you find yourself sharing a tiny changing room/toilet/bathroom with other performers, you may not have space to blow your balloons!

- How will you blow the balloons? You can use a pump or do it yourself, but bare in mind that if you want to hide glitter in the balloons for maximum effect when they pop, you will be better off using a pump as to avoid any wetness.

- What happens to the burst balloons? Whilst you can leave them in place after bursting them, this might ruin the aspect of your costume/underwear underneath. Ideally, tie the balloons to a piece of string or elastic that you can easily remove once the balloon is popped.

- What if the balloon refuses to pop? It might happen, after all, on stage mishaps are part of the business! If a stubborn balloon refuses to pop the first time, don't panic, just strike a pose, pull an "oops" face or a cheeky smile, and try again. As long as you stay composed, a balloon not popping at the first try will not ruin your act!

- Hit that beat! The best Balloon Pop routines I've seen were those that the performer had perfectly timed to the music used. One of my favorite Balloon Pop routine is the highly humoristic Balloon Pop Kiss by Good Ness Gracious. Each pop works perfectly with the timing of the music.

A Balloon Pop routine doesn't have to be classic, you can make it your own, make it funny, use an original song, tell a story... don't forget the preparation basics, and have fun with it! You can even ask audience members to pop balloons for you if the stage allows for audience participation. It will also solve the issue of those particularly hard to reach balloons...

A timeless classic: The Art of Fan Dancing

I have already mentioned fan dances a few times in this book, and how could I not! Fan dances are the epitome of burlesque. Since Sally Rand first popularized the act with her oversized white ostrich fans and her flesh costume, fan dances acts have been a staple in burlesque events. There are been at least one fan dance in pretty much every burlesque show I've ever seen.

There again, like for the Balloon Pop, there are a few basics to learn before doing a fan dance routine, and then you can make it your own.

- A fan dance might be the most iconic and widely known burlesque routine over the world, and promoters often specifically look for fan dances when booking shows, so having one in your repertoire might help you get booked.

There are a few things to consider before starting. Firstly, big fans are HEAVY. Trust me on this! The first time I did a fan dance workshop with Aurora Galore my hands and harms hurt for days. Check out her "Avalanche" routine on YouTube, and bear in mind her huge fans are incredibly heavy: you'll be astonished.

For a beginner, bamboo staves are preferable, as they are much lighter. The downside is you cannot have as many layer of feathers put on them, as they wouldn't support the weight. Still, if you're just starting out, or if you want to include a small fan dance section in one of your act, getting Spadone feathers (male ostrich feathers) fans on bamboo staves is the cheapest and lightest option. This is also the best option is you want to do a very quick fan dance, as they will allow you to move faster.

Now if you want that glamorous, thick fan look, you want to look at triple or quadruple layers or ostrich fans. Those will not hold on bamboo staves, and you will probably have to get plastic one: much sturdier, but also more difficult to handle, and certainly painful at first. On the plus side, they will look fantastic. The classic burlesque stars such as Sally Rand and Faith Bacon used the luxury version of ostrich fans, with ostrich feather boas. This is also what Dita Von Teese and Catherine D' Lish use, as well as Michelle L'Amour in her famous Sally Rand tribute act. They will take you more time to get accustomed to, and you will need to move slower, but they certainly have that glamorous star quality.

- Quality vs Price: Be aware that good quality feather fans are expensive. Whilst you can get a pair for around $100, they will certainly not be triple layered ostrich fans like professional use. It's fine if you're just starting out and you want to try out fans, or if you just want to integrate fans towards the end of your routine for a quick fan dance reveal, but don't expect them to have the same impact as more expensive fans. If your intention is to do a Sally Rand style classic routine, with slow, sensual moves, then you might need to think about investing more.

- How to use your fans: there are many ways you can integrate fans in a routine. You can do a full fan dance routine, where the focus will be on your dancing and ability and handling the fans for most of the routine. Performers who execute this type of routine typically only wear a nude costume, or pasties and a merkin or G-string underneath, and use the fans to conceal themselves for the major part of the routine. The whole act then relies on the tease and on the performer's moves. This type of act is very traditional and often booked by promoters for its glamorous value, but it will not work if your fans are cheap and lack coverage, or if you don't know how to use them.

Another popular option is the fan dance as a way to end an act. In this case, the performer will often strip to their underwear, then pick up the fans and tease the audience for a bit longer, usually removing their bra whilst doing the fan dance, and finally doing the big reveal at the end. Sometimes the dance will go on for a bit longer after the reveal.

- Fan dances do not have to be classic, you can make them your own in a variety of ways. For example, you could chose to use something other than fans, like Scarlet Rose and her fan dance performed with rose petals. Or you could pick fans in a different color or type of feathers, like Miss Twilight Sparkly and her peacock fan dance. Sukki Singapora uses traditional Asian fans instead of feathers.

Finally, if you want to get an idea of which moves you could do with big fans, or simply to add a bit of glam and feathers to your routine, you can also buy mini feather fans. These are often used in burlesque lessons to teach the students various moves and poses, and they can be integrated in group or solo routine.

Dita's specialty: The Glass Routine, a few tips

Now for another renowned burlesque routine... I give you the Martini glass act. You have probably heard of the Martini glass routine as it has been widely popularized by Dita Von Teese, but if she certainly is the most famous performer to use a glass prop, she is not the only one. Catherine D' Lish performs in a champagne glass and even has a duet routine with Dita. The oversized glass routine has become so popular, that now many companies offer to book a glass for corporate events and then book burlesque dancers to perform inside them. If you start getting booked for corporate or fashion event, this might be something you will be offered to do, so here's a few tips in case you ever perform in a giant glass.

First of all... be careful! These glasses are really high and really slippery. It might seem like fun and games, and you might think it's easy to look glamorous whilst splashing in a beautiful oversized champagne or martini glass, but I would actually not recommend accepting this kind of gig unless you're sure you can dance in a rather perilous setting and are a bit more experienced.

If you look at one of Dita Von Teese's glass routines for example, she often stands, bends, and performs many intricate poses in and out of the glass, and even on the border of the glass. This requires both strength and flexibility, as well as a good footing, and enough experience to look graceful and make it look casy.

If you become a professional burlesque dancer and you fancy getting your own giant glass, remember as usual to make the routine your own. The Martini glass routine is a trademark, and it might be hard to perform an original routine with this prop. Miss Carrie Ann for example, performs the routine as a Dita tribute.

On the other hand, nothing prevents you from offering your own original take on the idea! Sukki Singapora had a giant engagement ring built, with a mini pool in lieu of a diamond, thus creating a new, original act, based on the same classic idea. Velma Von Bon Bon offers her own comedy vision of the oversized glass act: she feigns to discover her new prop's measurements are slightly off, before launching into an acrobatic and hilarious routine to reach it.

Bear in mind that this kind of prop is more appropriate for dancers who have a bit more experience, and don't forget the practical considerations. A large prop will need to be transported to the venues... it might also be unsuitable for smaller venues, but we will get back to these points in the props section.

We've seen the basics, you know where burlesque came from and you've learnt a few famous names, you've discovered some classic routines and have an idea of different styles. It's time to think about taking your own first steps into the world of performance.

Chapter 2: Your first steps, how to create your first burlesque routine

There are various ways to start into burlesque. If you don't know anybody in the industry, you might be lost as to where to start, but fear not, we are going to have a look at a few options together.

Where do I start?

The group classes route

- Taking burlesque classes is a good way to start, especially if you're still unsure of the kind of performer you would like to be, or even if you don't know if you would like to go on stage yourself one day but enjoy the art form. It's also a less daunting option, as you will be with other beginners in the same situation as you, and you will have an experienced teacher guiding you. Finally, burlesque classes are fun! You will meet like-minded people, and you will learn the tricks of the trade in a warm, friendly setting. Whether you decide to try on your own or with friends, you will not be alone and you will get to test your newly acquired burlesque skills among other newbies.

Group classes are actually how I started into burlesque myself: there used to be a burlesque troupe called Etrois in the north-east of England, and the head performer Lou Lou Rocket would teach weekly beginners classes.

Usually you don't actually do any real stripping during your first few classes, sometimes you don't even do any real stripping until you get to an intermediate class, so this is a good way to dip a toe and see how you feel about stripping in front of an audience.

The teacher is typically a professional burlesque dancer with a few years' experience and will be able to guide you through the basics: walking, posing, pouting... The first few classes will usually be a bit of a "taster" during which you will learn some classic burlesque tricks, how to walk like a burlesque star, how to pose for a few seconds in a graceful manner, basically showing you how to hold an audience captive but also more technical tricks. For example, you might learn of to take off your stockings – you won't believe how many ways there are!, your bra, your dress...

Often the teacher will ask you to bring an extra bra to wear on top of yours or above your top, or other extra items of clothing you can wear of top of your own, in order to learn the moves without actually showing anything. This way you will slowly overcome any fear you might have, surrounded by other people in the same situation as you.

Your teacher might then choose to teach you a full burlesque routine they will have come up with for the group. I still remember the first full burlesque routine I learnt, to the tune of "Diamonds are forever" from the James Bond soundtrack. It was a very slow, sultry routine, involving peeling off long gloves.

Your teacher might also help you come up with your own routine. Often, this will be once you've already completed a beginners' course and you've already learnt the basics. I'm not speaking about all burlesque schools over the world as there are as many methods as there are teachers, but typically once you've been through one or more beginners' classes, you will have the option to try out more advanced options. For example, the teacher might ask you to think about a routine in a smaller group. My first routine as part as a small group involved 5 girls, and we decided on a song from the musical Chicago.

If you're ready to move on to solo routines, your teacher may guide you and help you rehearse your first performance.

Some schools offer beginner and improver classes: in improver classes you might learn to develop your own style and routine, your burlesque persona, with the aim to get your ready to go on stage solo. You may also have the option to take part in student showcases, as part of a big group, or on your own.

I will give a few addresses in the address section of this book, but you can also enquire about burlesque classes in your area by looking online, or asking local performers how they started and whether they also teach classes.

The solo path

- Starting solo, without the help of a teacher, might be a bit more daunting, but it's sometimes the only option if there are no classes in your area. It's also the best option if you already know a fair bit about burlesque, and have a good idea of what kind of performances you want to do already. Maybe you've already been to many shows, or you know burlesque performers and they've encouraged you to take that extra step. Maybe you've learnt it all online via online tutorials or by watching videos. Either way, what you lose in guidance you will earn in freedom.

If you decide to start on your own, it's even more important to do your research before starting. Watch as many videos as you can, watch as many videos as you can, read books on the subject. See how the professionals do it, observe their styles and learn. Find out which styles you prefer, and which you could see yourself performing.

Since you will be starting on your own, you're free to choose any song and any style for your first routine, so go wild, but remember a few basics. Find a large enough space to rehearse, preferably with wooden floors and a mirror. Stages (usually!) won't have carpet. Observe what your moves look like in the mirror. Ideally, film yourself or ask a friend to film you so that you can see what your routine will look like from the audience's point of view.

Pick a theme

- Some famous routines have a very clear theme and will help people remembering the performer. Your theme can be pretty much anything you choose! Perle Noire is most famous for her dance homage to Josephine Baker, "La Baker", Vicky Butterfly is known for her routines featuring giant props such as La Lune with a moon crescent, Anna Fur Laxi for her Bettie Page routine, Scarlet Rose for her streetlight routine...

The list of ideas is pretty much endless: historical or fictional characters, movies, books, games, anything! It's very important that you have a look around and know what routines are already out there by going to shows and watching videos. You don't want to start practicing a routine and then realize someone else has already been performing the same style of routines for years.

You can do a routine on a theme that's already been done of course, just make sure you're original and never copy someone else's routine.

There are different options for your routine: you could tell a story and / or play a character; you could have a general theme; or you can go for a classic Showgirl display.

If you want to tell a story or play a character, don't get on stage and start stripping, try to show why you're stripping: maybe you've spilt something on yourself, or you want to seduce someone (the audience), or you want to symbolize changing into someone else (by starting dressed innocently then reveals something sexier underneath)...

You don't have to tell a story, you can also go for the classic Showgirl route, or have a general theme like "nature", "fetish", "fairy-tales"... just be careful not to do something that's already been done too many times. There are many very similar fan dances performed to the same style of music and using the same moves for example. If you're going to perform your own fan dance, try to bring your personal touch. Originality is key to become a professional!

The all important music choice

Beware of traditional song choices...

- Your music choice should match your routine and your style, so pick carefully! Some songs are overused in burlesque, so unless a particular song really suits your routine perfectly, or you've always dreamt of performing to it, try to be original. There are already thousands of routine using "The Stripper"by David Rose & His Orchestra.

You will also have to listen to this song a lot... so make sure you really love it and don't just pick it because you think this is what the audience/promoters want to hear! I don't think I'll ever listened to "It's oh so quiet" by Bjork in the same way again after rehearsing a routine to it for months.

For classic, showgirl burlesque, have a listen to vintage music; jazz covers of popular songs are also a winner: it gives the audience something recognizable without being too obvious!

For neo-burlesque, anything song choice can work, as long as it makes sense with your routine!

Popular routines

Some routine themes are sure to be in high demand regularly and might help you get booked at the beginning.

Halloween and Christmas routines

Many professional burlesque dancers have a Halloween and a Christmas routine, or at least routines that may work in a Halloween or Christmas themed show. It doesn't have to be outright obvious – you don't need to go on stage dressed like a sexy pumpkin to have a Halloween routine, nor do you have to dress as a naughty Santa for Christmas. Anything dark or horror themed might be appropriate on Halloween, and a winter style routine could be appropriate for Christmas. For example, Trixie Blue has a Jack Frost themed routine for the end of the year; Miss Twilight Sparkle's "The Ritual" works very well for Halloween...

Halloween and Christmas are popular times, Halloween events especially are often the most successful in the year, and promoters/organizers always look for on-theme routines.

Whether you start as part of a group class or on your own at home, don't be scared to jump at the occasion whenever you see a workshop not far from where you are at the time. Even professionals can beneficiate from learning new skills, or new takes on classic skills, from others. Burlesque performance is a work continuously in progress, and you will soon realize that your first routines will look very different a few years on.

Burlesque walks and poses

Something you will definitely learn in any burlesque class is how to walk, how to pose, and how to take off various items of clothing. Even if you decide to start at home, it's worth going through the basics.

So you think you know how to walk?

Think again! To learn to burlesque you will have to learn a few of these classic walks... I don't aim to give an exhaustive list, and some of these walks might have different names depending on where you learn them, but let's have a look at the main ones. The names I use are those I learnt from my first burlesque teacher at

Etrois, you might know them under different designations.

- Revolver: Revolver is basically a sexy way to turn. Your non-dominant leg is slightly bent, your non-dominant foot on your tippy-toes, and your hips create a "rolling" motion. Your dominant leg follows the movement given by your other leg and your hips. You can do a half turn or a full turn over yourself using this move, "revolving" around yourself slowly, giving time to the audience to admire you.

- Showgirl: This is very similar to the walk models use on the catwalk, but with an exaggerated hip motion. Put one foot in front of the other as if you were walking on a straight line, and push your hips towards the opposite side. For example, when putting your left foot forward, push your hips towards the right.

Another version of this walk consists in dragging the foot at the back slowly towards the front on your tippy toes, slowing down the walk dramatically. This walk is best used at the beginning of a routine, when you're still fully dressed for example. If you have a big, intricate costume, it also gives plenty of time to the audience to admire it (and hides the fact you may not be able to move much before stripping down a few layers!)

- Show Pony: Another version of the Showgirl walk, this time you also pull your knee up at each step, in the manner of a... show pony. This walk can be used if your routine includes a riding crop for maximum effect, and is best done with a falsely stern face for a dominating effect – but of course you can make it your own and use it as you wish!

These are just a few of the burlesque style walks you might learn in a class, but there are many other, and not every performer will use the same names for them. Now let's have a look at poses...

Game face on!

- Poses and faces are often the hardest part when you first start burlesque! Whereas once you've performed for a while they will come naturally, you might find yourself giggling uncontrollably when you start practicing your best "sexy" or "coy" faces.

One pose we used to practice in my burlesque group was the "Look at my shoe!" pose... It consisted in stopping mid-walk, then bringing one of your leg forward, and point at your shoe! It aimed to teach us how to do "cute" and how to perfect that falsely surprised face when one item of clothing comes off... we would all shout "Look at my shoe!" at the same time, with an emphasis on the "shoe" for that round mouth effect, then giggle for five minutes. It's easy to feel silly when practicing poses, pouts and faces, but remember: on-stage, everything has to be bigger than life. Just like in theatre, if you don't exaggerate your facial expressions, the audience might not see anything! And in the true tradition of vaudeville, burlesque facial expressions are often *very* exaggerated.

- Let's consider a few "faces" and pouts you might learn in a burlesque class, or see burlesque performers doing. Obviously, burlesque "faces" will vary widely depending on who does them!

To start with the obvious, there's the "sexy" and the "sultry" pout. These are of course highly suggestive, and your teacher might show you a few options: open-mouthed, biting your lip, winking... or you might observe some professional burlesque performers and instead of watching just their dance moves, look at what their faces are doing.

There's the "cute" face, or "cheesecake" face. This is the one you will often see performers pull when they pretend to have accidentally dropped an item of clothing, or accidentally flashed a bit of skin to the audience.

Then there's the "stern" look, which might work better if your routine involves you playing a dominant character. Check out routines where performers play dominatrix characters but not only, it also works to play stern to play with the audience, as if to pretend you're not about to give them what they want (i.e.: you think I'm about to take this off? Think again!). It also works very well for any army/navy/school teacher inspired routine.

There is of course an incredible variety of faces and pouts a performer might do, the essential thing is to be larger than life. Think your facial expressions will have to be seen and understood by the audience, and they might not be close to you.

That's it for the very basics, now all you have to decide is which route you will choose to start into burlesque.

Will you venture into a class, a workshop, or will you try to go for it alone? Whichever route you prefer, just make sure it is what you feel comfortable with. Some people blossom inside a troupe, some people prefer to do things their own way, and both options are perfectly valid.

Now onto our next step! You might have an idea of where to start, and you know a bit more about burlesque walks and poses. You might have even started practicing in front of a mirror at home. Let's move on to another important part of the business. Whichever route you might have chosen to begin with, there are still a lot of essential things you need to know and learn to become a professional dancer.

What strikes you when you go to a burlesque show, or watch burlesque movies and videos? The dancers do not look like people you see in the street everyday. The costumes, the hair, the make-up: everything works together to create a larger than life burlesque persona. In our next chapter, we will consider a few tips to learn how to look your best when you first decide to step on stage.

Chapter 3: Costumes, glitter and DIY

Burlesque dancers must make the audience dream. If you want to be a professional performer, you have to give your audience something they don't see in everyday life. Unless your act involves you not looking glamorous (I would highly recommend checking out Tooshie La Ta Ta in her Hettie remembers routine for example: she plays an elderly woman in a hilarious comedy routine!), then stepping on-stage should be the occasion to look the part, whether that means looking like the most glamorous version of yourself, or looking like a completely different persona you've created.

You don't need to be the fittest, slimmest nor the most conventionally pretty girl in the room. That's the beauty of burlesque, all bodies and physiques are accepted. However you need to look the part, and that means not stepping on the stage like you would step out to do your food shopping, not even like you would dress for a night out.

Burlesque is all about performance, everything has to be bigger and shinier than in everyday life. Bigger hair, bigger lashes, shinier outfits.

Professional burlesque dancers know all the tricks to make themselves look a million dollar before they step on the stage. You can learn too and soon you'll learn to dazzle like Dita herself!

Your first burlesque outfit

- Your first burlesque outfit might be pretty basic. It all depends where and how you start, so for the next couple of paragraphs, let's assume you went with the group classes option, with a professional burlesque dancer as a teacher, or with a workshop option. You might not know if you ever intend to step on a stage yet, it could be your first lesson. No teacher will ask you to spend all your hard-earned money in a brand new outfit for a beginners' class, and often you will find you already have the basics at home (even more so if you're into vintage style).

- To start with: anything that might be stripped or peeled easily and sexily is your friend! You rarely see burlesque dancers wearing trousers on-stage for example (with the exception of trousers that can be ripped at once), as they are a bit difficult to remove nicely! This is the same reason why typically, any top worn on stage will have buttons, lace or a zip at the front: try taking off a turtleneck in a sensual manner. Of course it depends on the effect you're looking for, but my goal here is to give you a general overview. At the beginning, stick to things you won't get stuck in, skirts, shirts, blouses, buttoned dresses...

This is for the outerwear part... now for what you might want to wear underneath, let's explore a few common items.

Underwear, heels and corsets

- As I explained earlier, usually you won't even have to strip for your first few classes, you might only "pretend" and take off additional underwear, sometimes knickers, so at the beginning you will possibly use whatever lingerie you already have to test the moves out. However, this won't do to go on stage later on and you might want to either invest in some showgirl underwear – addresses to follow later in this book, or pimp your own with some DIY glitter/tassels/feathers, etc.

- You probably have some heels at home, don't be scared to dig out your fanciest pair! As far as height goes, different performers have different tastes. Dita Von Teese has her bespoke Louboutins, Toxic Cherry performs in 7 inches pleaser shoes, Betsy Rose Royal has a whole routine en pointe... it comes down to the style of routine you choose. Many performers also opt for ballroom dance shoes so that they're free to dance and still look glamorous in high heels. I would still recommend wearing high heels to get used to dancing in them. Performers make it look easy but you might feel like Bambi on ice at first!

- Corset/waist-clincher. Now there's one part of your first outfit you might not be familiar with. Corsets are the ones that cover your waist and breast, whereas waist clinchers as the name indicates, stop underneath. Again, if you're starting with classes or a workshop, you might not have one at first. I remember when I took my first burlesque lessons, my teacher Lou Lou Locket would show us how to take off a corset, and I'd try to reproduce the moves without having one in the first few weeks. The first corset I got was pretty cheap, black with some white lace, and the first few times I tried to take it off whilst dancing I got stuck midway... so if you intend to practice burlesque seriously, I'd definitely recommend getting a corset or waist-clincher from the start! Now not all burlesque dancers use corsets in their routines, but it is definitely a staple. Not only do corsets and waist-clinchers make your figure stand out, but it's also an item that can be removed in various interesting manners – playing with the bow at the back, toying with the audience by removing the front slowly or on time with the music, playing hide and seek once the corset is open...

Don't be tempted by a pretty but cheap option to perform on stage! You can find corsets very cheap corsets online, but they will have plastic underwiring. That's fine to learn how to take off a corset in class, but cheap corsets don't last long on stage. I made the mistake of buying a beautiful corset with plastic underwiring for a routine – the color was perfect to match the rest of my outfit, exactly what I was looking for! I think I only wore twice on-stage before the underwiring starting poking through the fabric (granted the routine was pretty energetic!). On top of that, it really hurt as it poked my skin too whilst dancing. Ideally you want to get a steel-boned corset. You can find decent options around £50/$70 these days, but a good corset can set you back double that, and a customized option usually starts around £200/$300.

Suspenders and Stockings... and nipples pasties

Another item you might not necessarily have in your wardrobe and another burlesque staple. If you take burlesque lessons or go to a workshop, I can guarantee you will learn how to take off stockings. Again, not all performers choose to remove stockings on-stage (at the risk of repeating myself, there are almost as many styles of routines as there are performers), but stocking removal is definitely part of a vast majority of routines. They are incredibly versatile on-stage: you may remove them slowly and sensually, play with the beat of the song, tease the audience, show off your flexibility, do it standing up, sitting down, whilst doing the splits... if you take classes you will probably learn tricks to remove them in a variety of ways you never imagined.

Now suspenders and stockings are the classic get-up, this is what the burlesque stars wore during the Golden Era, and if you want to go for a classic, Showgirl feel, you might want to opt for this option. Suspenders are of course compulsory if you wear stockings, and they will add a sexy vintage feel to your routine. Many performers also choose to wear hold-ups these days – less vintage but easier to keep up... At the beginning you might want to try both and see how you feel!

- Nipple tassels / Pasties. OK now if these are your first steps into the world of burlesque, it's likely you don't have those in your wardrobe. Nipple tassels or pasties are these little patches burlesque dancers wear on their nipples, as the names indicates. They were invented in the 1950s to circumvent strict morality laws. Ziegfield dancer and burlesque legend Carrie Finnell is credited for first adding tassels to her pasties and making them twirl - tassel twirling is still part of many routines to this day. Nowadays, they are not only worn to hide, pasties and tassels are an integral part of a costume. You can buy them ready-made, or you can order custom pasties or tassels to match your outfit. You can even learn how to make your own with tutorials and a lot of patience! If you're taking classes, your teacher might lend you some to try on a t-shirt. I think we learnt about tassel-twirling after a few classes when I first started. If you're starting on your own, get yourself a pair a try to spin them: it's not as easy as it sounds but once mastered you'll definitely want to throw some twirling into your routines!

- Props. Toy with a few small props to start with, if you're taking lessons your teacher might tell you what to bring or lend you some items. The first burlesque prop I played with in class was a tiny feathered fan.

Gloves are also a rather common item of clothing in burlesque class and on-stage. Anything you might be able to peel to make the tease last! Long gloves that go over your elbow look great and like stocking, are very versatile in a routine. You can take them off slowly, finger by finger, using your hands or your mouth... the most important thing is to check that they fit just right when you buy them, else you might get stuck or lose one before the chosen moment.

You might want to play with hats also, or your teacher might suggest you bring one. A hat can be a brilliant accessory in a routine, allowing you to pick it up to hide or reveal, just like you would do with a small fan.

This list is non-exhaustive, but it aims to give you an idea of what to expect during your first few burlesque lessons, or if you've learning at home, it will help you figuring out where to start costume-wise. Of course, the more you feel confident, the more you learn and the more you grow as a performer, the more your on-stage outfit might look completely different from this "beginner's starter kit". To give you a personal example, my very first on-stage outfit consisted in a zip-up skirt, suspenders and stockings, a corset and nipple tassels; one of my last routines involved a gigantic tutu, an elaborate LED cake hair-piece and long floating feathered cuffs! Be as creative as you want!

__Burlesque finances: How to cover your costs and learn to DIY!__

- DIY is a burlesque dancer's best friend! Unless you can afford to spend hundreds or thousands on costumes, learning a few tricks to make your outfits stand out is a must. A burlesque routine takes time to develop if you want it to be at a professional level, and both your moves and costumes must be stage ready. People who come to a burlesque show want to see something they don't see in everyday life, but no worries, you can learn to sell them the dream even if you're on a budget!

Being a professional burlesque dancer is not all glamour and parties: for a 4-5 minutes routine performed on-stage, there are months spent in rehearsals and working on an outfit and props. Like with any profession, burlesque dancers have to take into account financial realities. If you have some funds dedicated to starting your burlesque career then you can hire other people (seamstresses, head piece makers, people who embellish shoes and tassels...) to help your vision come to life; otherwise, get ready to make the acquaintance of glue guns and sewing machines! A customized corset can easily set you back a few hundreds, and embellishing anything with Swarovski crystals will look amazing but takes a lot of time – something that is reflected in the cost if you have it made for you.

Making their own costume is actually part of the fun for many performers. Besides, it allows you to express your creativity and to update your outfit or fix it if needed without having to go to someone to do it every time. DIY is also a way to make your costume stand-out from the crowd and to really let your burlesque personality shine through.

A few tips to keep the costs down

- Now for some basic financial advice to start your burlesque career. Nothing scary, just a few tips to keep in mind!

Whilst to start with you will probably only have one routine to perform as a newcomer, you need to have a set of a few different routines for promoters to book once you start working as a dancer professionally. That means a different costume for each routine. Now, if you're just starting, best focus on making your first outfit as beautiful and professional as possible, but don't forget every costume will need the same time and care. Don't forget the costume has to "pay for itself" in the long run. If you constantly create new routines with new expensive costumes, burlesque will be a (rather expensive) hobby, but if you want to work as a burlesque dancer, you need to keep costs in mind so that you don't end up in debt!

For example, if your first costume ends up costing $300 for basic materials, $150 in rhinestones, and $30 in sewing material, you will need to make $480 before you actually start making money. This is taking the costume only into account, and not the hours you've spent rehearsing the routine, nor the room you might have rented to rehearse in if you don't have space at home, and it doesn't take transportation costs into account either.

Even if you perform in your hometown, you will probably have to take a few buses or taxis/car in case of big props or late night finish. If you perform away, you will have to take into account train or plane costs – those can be covered by the promoters but not always, so keep track of your accounting! Then you might want to invest into a professional website and business cards, which entails having professional pictures taken.

A lot of photographers offer TFP (time for print) deals but if you want something specific, or pictures of your acts/you in your costumes, you might have to hire someone specifically.

You might not earn much for each show at first, until you start having some experience, a performer cv and videos to show, and a bit of a following. Let's say you make $70 per show, in the example above, your costume will have paid for itself after 7 shows – without taking additional costs like transport, time and marketing into account.

Of course there is the old saying "You have to spend money to make money"... but you might want to keep the spending reasonable. You might be looking at big burlesque stars like Immodesty Blaize and dream about her dazzling corsets and feathered head pieces, and you might already be picturing yourself riding a giant rocking horse or dancing on top of a human-sized customized vintage phone, but nobody gets to that level without time and work.

Also, you might not realize but costumes suffer through quite a lot on-stage and you will definitely have to make some reparations eventually! You might find yourself having to fix bits of your costume even before you've worn it on-stage for the first time! Burlesque dancing can take its toll on fragile showgirls outfits, and it's quite common for performers to always have a couple of needles and thread or fabric glue in their suitcases.

Then there is the washing issue: if you don't want to damage fragile feathered/sequined/rhinestones outfits, you might want to consider dry-cleaning (check beforehand that they don't use too high a temperature which might melt the glue/plastic etc.!).

There again, that's something to factor into your costume budget. One of my burlesque costumes has so many hand-sewn tassels that it can only be very gently hand-washed in warmish water and dried flat. No matter how much you take care of your costumes, some items will have to be replaced overtime, and you will definitely go through more stockings and hold-ups than you ever thought was possible.

Retiring or revamping a routine.

After a few years, you might not enjoy performing some of your first routines anymore, and you will want to retire or revamp them. Updating and constantly improving on routines and costumes is part of the job, if you watch the same routine from the same performer a few years apart, I can almost guarantee you will be surprised by the differences!

A very well-made, very well sewn/crafted costume might be sold to another performer if you want to retire the routine completely and the outfit is too specific to be used for another one, but a lot of the time, you can mix and match and reuse items from one routine to the other. I used to have a Batman inspired routine which I started performing with cheap costume shop wings I'd customized and an all-black corset. A couple of years later, I'd upgraded to Isis wings and a fully rhinestoned corset. Routines are alive, they change with you overtime.

My advice? Start with one well-crafted routine and costume, and build from there. Investing in a sewing machine can be a lifesaver to make and fix your costumes, you can watch a few YouTube tutorials or take a few classes if you have no idea how to sew. If sewing really isn't your thing, don't worry, there are many ways to make a burlesque costume, which we are going to see together.

Tips on making your own costumes from scratch

- You can make a burlesque costume almost from scratch, without prior knowledge and without breaking the bank. You just need time and patience, and a lot of creativity!

Let's start with the basics: your costume needs to match the feel of your routine, and you need to be able to move in it – it seems obvious but it's rather important! I made the mistake of having the most incredible headpiece made by a local milliner especially for a routine, one of my biggest costume splurge. Sadly the heaviness of the piece made it rather unstable, and despite my best efforts to make it hold on top of my head, it left me having to review my whole routine so that it wouldn't fall before the end...

Think about the feel you want to give to your routine, and consider a color scheme. Let's see two very different routine from the same performer as an example: Katrina Darling's God Save the Queen and Back to Black routine. One is a cheeky nod to UK royalty, the other is a dark, slow number. What would you usually associate with UK royalty? I'm guessing you're thinking crowns, Union Jack flags and red/golden colors, am I right? Well that's exactly what the performer went for with her costume. For her second piece to Amy Winehouse's Back to Black, I'll let you guess what kind of color scheme she went for...

One piece of advice I heard from my burlesque teacher 7 years ago: the costume should come after the routine. If you start creating a whole routine just to use a costume item you like, you might end up trying to make the routine fit together around it clumsily and lose track of the important. Once you know what routine you want to do, once you know the theme, the song, then you can start tailoring your outfit to complement your routine, not the other way.

A few examples: if you want to do an absinthe fairy inspired routine, you might want to consider shades of green, for a film noir inspired performance, you could study what 1940s actresses wore, for a devil themed dance, you would use lots of red and orange and other fire-inspired colors and items... it doesn't matter what theme or story you want to show on-stage, everything and anything is allowed, just make sure your costume complements and enhances your routine.

- Now where to start? Let's say you're going with the absinthe fairy idea, you've got your routine idea and your song and you've started rehearsing. You've decided to go with a green theme, and you want green underwear, a green corset and a panel skirt, with matching sparkling heels. Nothing overly complicated, but you want it to look as good as possible, you're picturing something shiny and a bit 1920s decadence inspired. You could certainly buy those items, but if you want to truly make your costume personal, and look every inch the professional on stage, then I recommend customizing heavily.

- Sequins, rhinestones, crystals and glue guns: meet your new favorite tools. You will never see a professional burlesque performer with a simple set of matching underwear. For our green fairy idea for example, you could certainly buy a simple set of green underwear, or you could even simply dye a pretty white set to get the exact color you need. Though that might look great, it doesn't mean that's enough to be a costume. You have many options to make your costumes shine, let's go through a few ideas.

- How to make your costumes shine!

For underwear like for corsets or shoes, rhinestones or Swarovski crystals are a must. It's time consuming, but the result will be worth it! Swarovski crystals are expensive, but they shine and catch the light like nothing else, and are often used by burlesque performers. You can find them online for around $5 for 100 crystals (2 mm) – it doesn't seem like much, but bear in mind that you could need up to 6,000 2 mm crystals for one pair of shoes, and a lot more if you want to cover a whole corset! Rhinestones are less pricey, around 80 cents for 100, and will also add bling to your outfit. You can buy them in bulks in haberdasheries or online.

Then all you need is a glue gun or a fabric glue such as GemTac, and you'll be all set to start embellishing your underwear and corset. You can do the whole surface for maximum effect, or you can pick and choose sections to embellish. You can use one or more colors, or decide to create patterns, it's up to you. Just bear in mind that bras and bra straps often stretch a little when worn or you might have a bad surprise when trying your creation on!

A glue gun will make the rhinestone process easier, but get ready to spend a few hours of your time embellishing your costume. If you're using smaller stones such as the 2 mm ones, a glue gun might be tricky to use, as it's more suited to bigger flat stones. If you want to play with different sizes, you might have to work without for the smaller stones. For a first, I would suggest picking sections to embellish as covering the whole surface of a corset could take you around 100-150 hours, or around 30 hours for a pair of shoes - still using 2 mm crystals, bigger crystals will of course reduce the time spent, it all depends on the effect you're looking for! With 5 mm or 10 mm crystals, you could reduce the time by more than half, but you might have bigger gaps in between stones, even if you're very careful to glue them very close to each other.

Another tip: it'll be easier to glue rhinestones or Swarovski crystals over an item of a similar color, as the gaps in between crystals will be less noticeable. As for the technique, simply put the hot glue tube inside the glue gun and press gently until some glue comes out. Don't wait too long before gluing the stone to the desired surface or it might start setting.

For hand gluing, avoid Super Glue if possible: if you miss and put some on the rhinestone, it will dull its shine.

Rhinestones and Swarovski crystals are far from being the only embellishments you can use to get your outfit looking professionals. You could use beads or sequins on corsets and underwear for example. Those are better hand sewn so again, get ready to spend a bit of time applying them, but the result will be worth it! You can also go with a mix of materials for a unique style.

There's also the cheaper and faster glitter option if you're stretched for time and money. It will look great on-stage, however don't expect it to last quite as long, and you might have to do frequent touch-ups. You will need very fine glitter for better results.

The concept is simple: apply fabric glue to the desired surface – undergarments, shoes or corset, then powder with glitter. Don't forget to cover the areas you don't want to glitter with masking tape. You can also create shapes or highlight one part of the garment. Alternatively, for a more precise result, mix two third of glue and one third of sparkle and apply with a paintbrush. Add as many layers as necessary (and don't worry, the glue will become transparent once dry). Let it set, and apply strong hairspray or preferably an acrylic or polyurethane spray.

You could also use tassels, for example you could buy pretty curtain tassels from an haberdashery and sew them to a bra and thong to create the perfect bump and grind costume! Feathers also look amazing on burlesque costumes, glue them one by one or sew them so that they last longer.

A quick guide to making your own nipple tassels

You could also make your own nipple tassels or pasties to match your outfit. All you need to do so is a double sided sticky sheet, leatherette, a shiny material of your chosen color and whatever else you want to add to your pasties: feathers, bows, tassels so you can tassel twirl... Simply cut the desired shape into the sticky material – pasties are often round but heart shaped are also common, and many performers have customized pasties matching their acts. I used to have bat-shaped ones for my Batman inspired routine for example. Once the desired shape cut, stick leatherette to one side of the pasties, and the desired material to the other side.

The tricky part is to fold them so that they can be taped to your nipples later. For a circle shape, fold the pasties once horizontally, then once vertically. You should be able to see a bit of a cross shape on the leatherette (the back of the pasties). Cut along one of the lines, up to the middle of the pasties. You should have a perfect circle with one slit. put a tiny bit of glue on the front side by the slit, then glue the other side of the slit on top of it. This should have for effect to give your pasties the right shape to tape onto your nipples. Do try to fold without gluing at first.

Now you can decorate your pasties, go wild! You can use your glue gun again and use sequins, rhinestones, feathers... anything you like. If you want to include tassel twirling into your routine, don't forget to add one tassel in the middle!

Where to find the best burlesque outfits

OK, we've seen a few tips on how to make your own burlesque costumes, but what if you want something very specific, or complicated, and you're unable to do it yourself? There are many online shops dedicated to burlesque and showgirl costumes.

- Many performers also sell tassels, costumes, headdresses... check out your favorite performers' social networks and websites and discover a treasure trove! Here are a few who sell their goodies online:

There are often stalls at burlesque shows and they can be a mine to find original, hand-made burlesque accessories and to meet the creators and have a chat if you need something specific.

You can also research seamstresses in your area to help you with a particular outfit, or to reshape something you found on a vintage shop. On that note...

Vintage shops are your friends!

- Vintage shops are the go-to place and a mine of amazing costume ideas. It will also guarantee you will have something authentic and unique to wear on stage. If you're going for a vintage feel, get researching vintage shops in your area, and don't hesitate to visit vintage and second-hand shops wherever you go! The UK for example has incredible second-hand shops. I once found a 1940s suit I used in a teacher routine.

- Get creative with your finds: customize, resize, embellish... follow the same steps as above if you want to make your outfit shinier and more suited to the stage.

Chapter 4: Hair and make-up, channel your inner starlet

Now you've got the costume and you've been practicing your DIY skills, it's time to move on to the next step: hair and make-up. Don't be scared to overdo it, stage hair and make-up are meant to dazzle and be seen from the audience! Over the top doesn't exist in burlesque!

Hair and make-up are an important part of creating a professional burlesque act and to make an impression on your audience. It's not enough to have a perfectly crafted routine. Little things can sometimes bring an act down, you wouldn't see a professional performer without her nails done for example: it seems small but details like that make the difference between a professional and an amateur. Once you're onstage you're selling dream (unless you go for a comedy act). It would be a shame to rehearse an amazing routine and let it down by not paying attention to the details.

Classic Burlesque hairstyles: vintage goodness

- Doing your hair the same way you would on a normal office day won't do! Just like you wouldn't step onstage wearing your every day attire, if you want to truly look professional, you need to learn how to style your 'do and to apply make-up in a completely new way. Getting ready for a burlesque show takes time, though the more you do it, the quicker it will get.

There are also little tricks to go a bit faster, for example you can choose to wear a wig instead of doing your own hair.

Whether you choose to go for the vintage option, a wig or an elaborate hairpiece, the bigger the better! Many dancers go for a vintage do when they perform, as a way to reference performers of the Golden Era, but also simply because vintage hairstyles were glamorous and elaborate, they were made to complement women's facial features.

- As for your costume, you want your hairstyle to match the routine you're performing. This seems obvious but might be a bit tricky if you're booked to perform two or three routines in the same night!

In that case, you have a few options: if both your routines are in a similar style, for example if you mostly perform pin-up, showgirl, cheesecake routines, then the same style might work for both. Otherwise, try to not style your hair in a way that can't be easily undone for the following routine, i.e. don't overdo it on the hairspray and pins if you need to let your hair down.

If for one routine you need to have an up-do, and you want to let it down for another one, don't forget to factor the time you need to go from one to the other in your getting ready time backstage. If it's easier to go from up-do to letting your hair down and the schedule for the night is quite tight, maybe ask the promoter to do the up-do routine first. In any case, practice at home beforehand, and assume you won't have a lot of time to get ready for your second routine. A 30 minutes interval might seem like a lot, but it's really not when you have to change into an elaborate costume (new nipple tassels included), touch-up your make-up and sort out your hair!

- If you have no idea where to start when it comes to doing your hair, ask yourself a few questions: What suits me? What is the style of my routine? Who inspires me? Check out your favorite performers' styles, read online blogs about vintage styles, look at old videos and photographs and get inspired. If you want to do classic Showgirl or Cheesecake burlesque, a vintage hairdo is a must, but you can pick one that will complement your features. A vintage hairdo can mean anything from Bettie Page's straight fringe to Marilyn Monroe's curls.

Learn how to do your hair like a vintage vixen!

Hair pins are your new best friends – as you might have noticed by now, by getting into burlesque you're becoming familiar with an array of tools and items you might have never thought about using before!

Vintage hairdos rely on hairpins a lot to hold... and I mean a lot! The first time I got my hair styled in a vintage fashion during a workshop I was amazed at the quantity of pins used. I think I had to take out about 60 afterwards, and the 'do was pretty simple, 1950s curls. I used hairpins to make my wigs hold onstage also, in order to avoid losing it with an energetic moves. Basically: invest in lots of pins. If you're not familiar with them, they come in different colors in order to match your hair and be as invisible as possible from the audience's point of view.

Then get practicing! Nobody becomes good at something the first time, and you want to look great for your first show. Don't leave it to the last minute either, thinking you'll see about your hair and make-up on the day. Practice at home first, so that when the day of your first show comes, you already know what suits you and how to do it, and you don't spend precious hours running around trying to fix your hair and make-up last minute. You don't need the extra stress!

Besides, it takes time to learn how to do vintage hairstyles if that's what you're going for, and you might need some new accessories.

- Easy curls... An "easy" way to get pretty vintage curls is to use heated rolls, the kind you plug then leave in your hair for 10 minutes or so to get pretty waves, or up to an hour to get real curls. Though the heated rolls themselves are quite easy to use, you might need a few attempts before you get the desired result... I found out from experience. Depending on the length and texture of your hair, the results may vary wildly! My first attempt ended up with me sporting an over-curled fringe that had nothing vintage about it. The second attempt was wavy, in a beach style way. My point is: you learn through trial and error. Try things out, and see what timing and technique work best for you.

Victory rolls: A tutorial

Let's have a look at how to do one popular vintage hairdo, Victory rolls. This classic hairdo was invented in the 1940s, and consists in lots of curls framing the face, an effect achieved with a lot of hairspray and backcombing. It works best on long or medium-long hair, or on a wig (check first that the wig can be style and washed like natural hair or you might damage it).

- Let's go through a few steps and then you can get practicing at home! Victory rolls take a bit of time, but they're not the hardest vintage hairdo to achieve, which makes them a good choice for a beginner.

- Start by protecting your hair with an heat protection spray to avoid damaging it, then work in sections with a curler. A medium-size curler (19 mm for example) is ideal. After you curl each hair section, hold on to the curl, squeeze it, and pin it to your head.

- Repeat for each section until you have curls pinned all over your head, then allow them to cool down completely for 10 minutes.

- Let down all your curls, then brush them with a boar bristle brush. You should now have large vintage style waves.

- With a comb, create a side-parting. Once you have the side-parting, separate your hair from the middle up to behind your ear. Then on both sides, clip the rest of the hair away, only keep the front sections free.

- Divide the front hair into sections, and start teasing with a comb. Tease the hair section by section – don't take huge section at a time, this is the important part! Then get your boar bristle brush again, and smooth the outside of your hair out gently.

- You now have the base for your Victory rolls! Put a pin (grip) into place at the base of what will be your first Victory roll, just beside your parting, then start rolling the hair from the bottom with two fingers, thus leaving a space or tunnel in the middle of the hair. Once you reach the top of your head, firmly pin the roll – it should rest where the grip is.

- For maximum effect, do a second Victory roll with the other section.

Neo-burlesque style

Victory rolls and vintage styles are very popular, however looking like a 1950s Hollywood star is not compulsory to perform burlesque!

Plenty of neo-burlesque performers do use vintage styles, and depending on your burlesque persona and your routines, many other creative options are open to you.

If you're doing comedy burlesque for example, looking glamorous might not be your goal! Tooshie La Ta Ta's little old lady routine for example calls for a gray haired wig. And I once saw Vendetta Vain performing a poodle routine with a huge curly wig. Wigs in general are a fantastic way to be versatile, allow you to match your costume, and also mean less time spent on styling your hair!

Some wigs are even true works of art, such as the Arachnia Wigs created for Anna Fur Laxis or drag performer Kim Chi.

As always, it all depends on you, what you want your burlesque persona to be like, and what works with your costume.

If you're lucky enough to have a long thick mane, you might want to consider light styling only, à la Trixie Blue or Sukki Singapora.

Accessorize, accessorize, accessorize!

Head pieces, hats, flowers, jewels... be creative and make your hair a work of art!

Have fun with your hair! If you go for a vintage style, you might want to add some bows, a fascinator, or even flowers to your 'do. For an exotic routine you might even consider fresh flowers, or why not a rose you an gift your audience later.

Fascinators are not only for weddings, in fact since discovering burlesque I found out there are many creators of bespoke and original fascinators. Check out Pearls & Swines and you will never see fascinators in the same way! You can get fascinators with birds, with fruit, with cake, with pretty much anything you can imagine. Just make sure you can dance with it on your head – a heavy head-piece might not be steady!

You've probably seen those gigantic feathered head-pieces famous dancers, showgirls and performers in Parisian Cabarets such as the Lido and the Moulin Rouge wear. They will look great, and if you perform as a duet or in a group they will certainly give that glamorous French vibe to the routine, but be aware that they're not cheap – just like feathered fans, and also quite warm and heavy!

Make-up addict

We've covered the hair – although there is still much, much more to discover, but a whole book would be needed to fully cover burlesque hairdos! Now let's have a look at stage make-up.

Make-up is a very important part of creating a professional burlesque persona. You can learn how to enhance your features, transform them, and match your make-up to the rest of your routine to look your best on stage.

You might not be familiar with performance make-up. When you see somebody on stage, you may not realize just how much make-up they wear, nor how much time they invested into getting ready. You just see performers looking glittery and fabulous, with defined features despite the blinding lights. These are all tricks that can be learnt be beware. Once you start diving into this world of contouring and glitter, you might not ever want to come out. Welcome to your new obsession!

Stage make-up: not your everyday attire

Stage make-up is NOT your usual make-up. You need to stand out. Things that might look "too much" in real-life will look amazing under the spotlights.

And what says "stage make-up" and conjures pictures of glamorous burlesque stars more than extravagant fake eyelashes? The first time I did my make-up for a show, I think I spent the best part of the afternoon learning how to put them on... If you've never tried applying fake eyelashes for a night out, I would suggest having a go before the big day! Once you get the hang of it, it can be done in seconds, but the first time it took me half an hour.

You could also get lashes extensions that last for a few weeks, but the fake eyelashes performers wear on stage are sometimes a lot more flamboyant than simple lashes! Don't be scared to overdo it with jeweled, feathered, or otherwise extravagant lashes. Primark has a surprisingly good selection, especially during the party season, so stock up!

- Why is stage make-up so heavy? Simply put, without heavy stage make-up, you would look as if you had no facial features at all, especially if the stage is a bit far from the audience. Both men and women dancers need make-up on their eyes and lips when performing. You need heavy eye make-up and fake eyelashes (or tons of mascara) to define your eyes, you need heavy lip make-up to define the contours of your lips, and unless you want your facial features to look flat under the spotlight, learning how to contour and highlight is a must. It might feel too much when you try it on at home but trust me, it's probably nowhere near enough.

- Powder is your friend if you're going to perform under spotlights. Those get really hot, and you don't want to be sweaty and shiny by the end of your performance. If you tend to get shiny and you don't want your make-up to run, use primer before applying your foundation, then loose powder all over your face once your make-up is done. You can also invest in a fixing spray... or use a tiny bit of hairspray on your face, just don't forget to close your eyes first! That last option is definitely not to be used everyday, but it works.

- For fuller lips, you can try to use a lip pencil in the same color as your lipstick to draw them bigger, or you can play with different colors of lip gloss. Apply a dark lipstick all over, then a lighter color in the middle so that your pout looks fuller, then blend with another lip gloss.

- Don't forget the brows! Unless not having brows works for your routine, or you want to style them in a 1940s style - check out Joe Black, the cabaret genius for a lesson in how to give perfect vintage brows – you need to accentuate your brows, or they'll disappear onstage.

- Dabbing some light eye-shadow, highlighter or powder in the inside corner of your eyes will make them dazzle and look bigger.

- Be careful to match the theme and feel of your routine! A classic vintage style make-up with red lips and eyeliner does work in most situations, but if you're going for something funny, or nerdy, or very cheesecake, you might want to adapt your make-up style.

If you're not sure what works best at first, try to stick to the basics and learn how to do them well: red lips (orangey reds for warm complexions, cooler shades of ruby reds against pale skins), black eyeliner, shaped brows, and... contour.

Contouring: a quick tutorial

Contouring is the most useful make-up trick you can learn! It will make your features stand-out from afar, give definition to your face, and even camouflage the areas you're not so fond of.

Contouring is a favorite on the burlesque and the drag scene. Let's have a look on how to contour like a pro in no time.

The best quick contouring trick I got was from Trixie Blue, put some darker foundation under your cheekbones, on the sides of your nose and on your chin, some lighter foundation on your cheekbones and on your nose, et voilà! It sounds easy, but it actually took me quite a while to master... so let's see a more detailed explanation.

- First, get the kit. You will need your usual foundation, which matches the color of your skin, and two more: one that's two shades darker than your usual foundation, and one that's two steps lighter. Ideally, choose stick foundations so that they're easier to blend. Many brands offer contouring kits nowadays so you're sure to find what you need.

- You can use a sponge or brush to blend, or just your fingers to start with.

- How to map your face: use the darker shade to trace your temples, narrow your nose (and shorten it if you wish), mark your cheekbones and define your chin.

The darker shade needs to be applied just above the hollow part of your cheekbones, on the sides of your nose for that narrowing effect, and on the tip to shorten it. On your temples, just trace them for light definition, or go all the way to your hairline if you want your forehead to look smaller.

You also need to apply the darker shade to your jaw line, under your chin, and put a tiny line just under your mouth – this will serve to make your pout stand out.

- Blend, blend, blend! Use small circular motions to blend the darker shade into your base foundation, then move on to the lighter shade.

- The lighter shade will serve to make your features pop, and will hide any sleep bag or dark circles. Apply it generously under your eyes, then put a tiny bit in the middle of your forehead, on the bridge of your nose, and on the chin. Blend again!

- Now fix it with loose powder. There you go, your face now looks more defined and stage ready!

Glitter fever: More is best!

Glitter is a staple in most burlesque shows. Performers put glitters on their costumes, pour glitters all over themselves, fill bottles of champagne with glitter, put glitter in the balloons they pop, more glitter in their hold-ups so that little shiny crystals fly when they peel them off, burlesque performers are never bored of glitter!

Glitter looks amazing on stage so learn to use it on your face and body too. If you plan to use glitter in your act however, don't forget to let the promoter know if the quantities are important as it will make the stage slippery for the next performer, and someone might have to clean it up.

- Mastering the art of glittery make-up is a must. One little trick for glittery lips that last: use eyelashes glue on your lips, then powder them with glitter. Just be careful not to bite your lips...

With that in mind, we conclude the fourth part of this book. You should now have a good idea of the type of burlesque dancer you'd like to be, you might have already started rehearsing your routines, and you've been practicing your hair and make up skills in front of your mirror... I guess all that's left is going into the world and performing in front of an audience!

Chapter 5: How to perform in your first show

This is it: your routine is ready, your costume couldn't be better, and you've mastered the art of burlesque hair and make-up. Now all that's left is finding your first show, and getting on that stage for the first time! A task that can be a bit daunting, even more so if you don't know anyone in the industry and you're starting out on your own. Don't worry, the burlesque scene is welcoming of newcomers, and with a few tips you will soon find your first occasion to shine.

Of course you need to make sure you absolutely ready before doing so, so don't skip on those rehearsals!

Rehearsals

- It seems obvious, but you need to know your routine by heart to prepare for your first show. Many seasoned professionals actually do improv' routines as well, just check out Beau Rocks doing some free style bump and grind on YouTube to see what I mean. However, in order to be able to freestyle, you need to be perfectly in control, you need to know yourself and have mastered the art of tease down to a T. When you first start out, it's best to have a routine you know so well, you can go through the moves without having to think about them. This, ironically, is how you will find the space to improvise and play with your audience.

If you're too focused on remembering the next move, you will not be able to relax, and you might miss out on audience interaction. You're also more likely to panic if you forget a move, so rehearse as much as possible, until you can't hear your song without going through the moves to yourself!

- Mirrors are your friends! If you don't have large mirrors at home, maybe consider renting a rehearsal space for a few hours. You could split the costs with other performers. Otherwise, ask a friend to film you, or position your phone or camera so that you can see yourself entirely from the audience's point of view.

Sometimes, you might try to reproduce a move you like, or you might think a step looks great, but it could look very different from the audience's point of view. Always keep in mind where the audience will be, but be ready to adapt. I once performed on an old-school round stage, and the audience was sat all around. Where I normally would tease and take off the front of my corset with my back to the audience, I had to change bits of my routine so that everyone could see.

In most venues however, you will have an audience side and a backstage side, so try to get a clear idea of what the audience will see. There are little things you might not have thought about, especially if you're starting on your own: for example, if you take off your hold-ups or stockings as part of floor work, don't forget to take off the stocking on the leg that's on the audience's side. Otherwise, they will miss a lot of the action!

Dressed rehearsals

Another point that might seem obvious, but will prove very important and will definitely go a long way to make you look professional: always rehearse in your costume a few times before the show.

- Can you dance in your costume? If you've worked out your whole routine before having the final outfit, you might find yourself needing to make some adjustments. For example, if you've timed your stocking removal perfectly to the beat of your song, it might not work as well if you're wearing a different pair. Or you might find yourself too constricted in your new corset, or find out it takes longer to remove than you thought.

- You might also have to make small adjustments depending on the venue: low ceilings are the enemy of big moves, so enquire about the venue size beforehand! You don't want your new fans to hit the ceiling, or to damage your gown by throwing it too high.

- Make adjustments if necessary: you can have the most beautiful costume ever, if you cannot move in it, your routine will suffer. I spent months planning a new routine inspired by Marie-Antoinette and cakes once. The costume looked exactly like what I imagined, and I was so happy with my giant cake-hat. It would light up too! I still ended up performing the routine very little as the whole outfit was rather impractical and I could barely move my head without risking the cake falling... I had to rework the whole routine, removing all floor work and focusing on slower moves for it to work. My point being: your costume and your routine should work together, so rehearse in it as much as possible, and correct any issue before the first show.

- Plan for mishaps and laddered stockings! You WILL ladder stockings or hold-ups whilst rehearsing, or on stage. It happens all the time, it's just part of the job, so stock up on stockings!

Mishaps also happen on stage, and you cannot possibly plan for everything. The best you can do is be prepared and know your routine by heart, so if a mishap happens on stage, you feel confident enough to improvise a bit and then go back to your routine. You might never had any trouble removing your corset, gown, skirt, a hundred times, and then you'll get to one hundred and one and get stuck. It happens to everyone, and if you end up having a career in burlesque, it will happen more than once. I had to break out a beautiful gown after it got tangled before. You might have to learn to fix things on the go too, so always carry some thread and needles with you! If you've got two shows in the same night and a piece of your costume comes undone during the first one, you might have to perform some quick repairs.

Ok, your routine is ready, you've rehearsed it so much you're actually doing the moves anytime you hear your song, and people give you funny looks in the metro because you pout your heart out mentally rehearsing with your mp3 player (true story). Now let's get you on that stage.

Student showcases

If you've been taking classes, it's likely there is the option to perform in a show, or a student showcase.

Burlesque student showcase

- Different burlesque teachers might offer different options to their students. If your teacher is part of a troupe, or if they organize shows regularly, they might suggest your perform in their show with the rest of your group. For example, when I started taking classes with Etrois, the troupe would put on a burlesque show every 3 months, and the students had the opportunity to perform a group routine. At the beginning, we would perform one routine taught by our teacher as a big group. Then as we all learnt more and developed our burlesque styles, we would perform as smaller groups and make up our own routines.

For me it was very progressive: first I performed a big taught group routine on stage, then a smaller group routine with a 20 seconds solo part, then I performed as a burlesque duo for a year or so. I'd already performed in shows for about 18 months before I got on stage alone for the first time. Depending on the class you choose, or how confident you feel, it might be very different for you.

Some classes, such as House of Trixie Blue's classes in the UK, offer beginners' courses to learn the basics, and more advanced classes giving the students the opportunity to perform, in this case as part of the Blue Belles (HoTB's student troupe) showcase, or even as a solo artist if you and your teacher think you're ready to take things one step further. Other burlesque schools all over the world offer similar classes, usually with an opt-in student showcase or the option to be part of the teacher's show.

- Student showcases are a good opportunity to see how you feel on stage in a safe environment, surrounded by friends and people you know. If you started as part of a student troupe/class, make the most of this opportunity to develop your style, and to learn how to feel confident on stage.

Of course student showcases are not paid, you pay for the class and for the guidance and opportunity to develop your stage skills. If you want to become a professional burlesque dancer, the next step is to find your first paid show. And if you started on your own, or if you took some online classes, your first experience onstage is likely to be solo, in a show where you'll be the newcomer or "newbie".

How to get booked

Whether you started as part of a class, or on your own, to become a professional you will need to start getting booked by promoters.

- If you've already taken part in showcases, you might find a slot by word of mouth. For example, another promoter/burlesque performer attended the show and would like to book you; or you have a chat with them and offer to do a newbie slot at their next event. Otherwise, you will have to apply to find shows.

Your burlesque CV

- Yes there is such thing as a burlesque CV. At the beginning you probably will not have much to put on there, but if you want to get booked, the minimum you need is a few pictures of your act(s) and a description. If you've never performed your routine onstage, get a few professional pictures taken in your costume. Ideally have a video ready to send, or a YouTube link to your routine. The video does not have to be top quality, especially if you're a newbie. The promoter just needs to see what they're booking. Try to give as much information as you can on the routine: theme, style, song, costume, where do you start (on stage or off?), what will need cleaning up from the stage (bra, tutu, glitter?).

- It's a good idea to have a little blurb ready about yourself. It's always a bit awkward to write flattering things about oneself, so if you struggle, ask a friend to help you! Your blurb should describe briefly, in a few lines, who you are as a performer. A mini biography giving the promoter an idea of who you are.

- Here are a few short excerpts from professional performers' websites[2]:

Roxy D' Lite: "Classic striptease with a modern twist is the hallmark of Roxi's performance style; (...)".

Scarlet Rose: "A Professional Provocateur both on and off stage, (...) her unrepentant love of bump and grind has even caused audience members to cry 'encore'".

Chrys Colombine: "Hailed as a "porcelain doll" and "burlesque goddess", the London-born showgirl is known for her unique, exquisite routines,(...)."

Trixie Blue: "This multi-award winning burlesque enchantress (...), Trixie blue, is highly acclaimed for her seductive prowess and jaw dropping performances."

Once you've performed a bit more, you can list a few shows you've performed at, and even add a few reviews your were given by the promoter or other performers. As you perform more and more, you won't be able to write down every show, so update your CV regularly with new routines and current location. Of course when you first start, your bio will be short, but as your career develops your can add famous events you performed at, or any award won.

---

[2] from the performers' own websites :
https://www.houseoftrixieblue.co.uk/trixieblue,
https://www.houseoftrixieblue.co.uk/enchantress-scarletrose, https://chryscolumbine.com/about-2/,
https://www.roxidlite.com/about

Look at performers' websites to get a better idea of what to write.

Later, you can get a website, or you might make (or have made for you) a video resume showing a few seconds of each or your routines.

Find events to perform at!

- Find shows in your area: that's the easy one if you live in a big city, or in a city where burlesque shows or events including burlesque happen on a regular basis. It might be easier if you live in the UK or in the US than in other countries though, but if you have the option, simply talk or write to promoters in your area.

Option 2 if you don't know of shows in your area (or there aren't any): find them online. Join Facebook groups for performers and newbie performers (for example try to type "burlesque performers in the US" or "burlesque UK", etc.). Promoters often post performance slots offers on their Facebook page or in groups. Don't be scared to send your CV directly to promoters even when they don't advertise, they might contact you for a later show. Big shows are often booked months or a year early, but by keeping your eyes open you might be able to jump on the occasion when a last-minute slot opens.

- Find out what styles a particular promoter tends to book and whether you'll be a good fit: some burlesque shows or events are very diverse, others will be geared towards something more specific. For example, if you only have one or two routines, and they're both rather classic showgirl burlesque, don't apply to a show with a fantasy theme.

- Being willing to travel is always a plus, open up your possibilities! If you live in a remote area or in a small town, you might not have a choice anyway. But even if you live in London or New York, you might want to explore other options. Besides, the more you travel for burlesque shows, the more performers and promoters you meet, and the more you're likely to get booked for other events. These things have a tendency to snowball.

The "newbie" slot

- Know that you might not get paid or paid much for your first couple of shows. It depends on the promoter's policy, often though promoters will offer to pay for your travel expenses within a reasonable limit (bus fare yes, plane tickets... not at the beginning). It's not rare for newbies to perform for travel expenses only or a small fee at the start. If you've never been on stage and have no videos and barely any picture to show, promoter will likely not want to take a gamble and spend much of the budget on someone they don't know.

- On the other hand, don't sell yourself short once you have a bit more experience. Find out what the usual fees are in your areas for new performers, and don't be lured by promoters asking you to perform in exchange for "exposure" once you've started getting paid. Granted, the balance is hard to find when you're just starting, because you do need to get your name out there, but don't forget that performing burlesque professionally is a job, and like every job, it deserves proper remuneration.

First time on stage

This is it, the big day has come and tonight you're performing on-stage for the first time! Here are a few tips to make this the best experience possible.

Last checks

Be prepared

- Check a few important points with the show organizer before the show:

- Will there be a stage-maid? A stage-maid (UK burlesque jargon) is the person who will clean up the stage after your routine. For example, the stage-maid will remove any garment you might have taken off from the stage and stage area and bring them to you backstage, so you don't have to run around half-naked picking up your clothes – you gotta admit it would ruin the glamour.

- Do you start on-stage or backstage? Let the promoter/DJ know! It's another very important point to mention, though the promoter should normally ask you. Let's say you've rehearsed your routine with an off-stage start, for example you've decided to walk from one side of the stage to the center glamorously over 15 seconds. If the person in charge of the music doesn't know and starts too late or too early, you might either find yourself waiting on the side of the stage whilst the audience wonders awkwardly what's happening, or you could end up running towards where you want to be.

- Can you transport your props on your own? Now this one might come a bit later in your career, unless you've decided to go big from the start and invested in/made a giant prop. It's all fine and dandy as long as you rehearse at home, but if you find yourself transporting a giant chair/ice cream cone/toy horse/glass... alone in the bus, it won't be quite as fun. Even smaller costumes and props can end up taking quite a bit of space. Don't leave packing until the last minute. Check that your costume and all your props fit comfortably in a suitcase or bag you can actually move around.

- Do you need someone to help you set up? That's another one to mention to the promoter and / or stage-maid, though they should normally ask you. It's best to mention the set-up when you first get booked. An example of set-up could be: Set up, one small table center stage, with a chair on the left (audience view), and a bunch of flowers on the chair. Or: Set up, pair of fans laid down center stage, audience side.

- If you're using glitter: ALWAYS let the organizer know beforehand. They might have to put you on before the break or to plan a quick clean up! Glitter looks fantastic but is incredibly slippery. Also, some venues do not accept large amounts of glitter to be poured on their floor.

A friend once poured an entire bottle of champagne worth of glitter on herself at the end of a routine, Flashdance-style. It looked frankly amazing and the venue never had any objection to glitter before then... as the carpets were going to be changed anyway. They'd just been changed. The new carpets were still glittering years later. Point is: always ask.

Scout the venue beforehand

Ok that might not be so practical if the venue is far from where you live, but if you can, then make the trip to check it out. Alternatively, have a look at the venue's gallery online, or ask the promoter to send you a couple of pictures if they have any from previous shows.

Know your surroundings

Here are a few things you need to find out- before the day of the show ideally, so you can adapt if needed:

- How big is the venue? Can you perform your routine as intended on the stage?

I mentioned that point briefly earlier, but if you've planned lots of big moves and the venue's ceiling is low, you might need to rework some parts of your routine at the last minute. Definitely check the ceiling height to avoid any bad surprises! Also, if you've rehearsed in a huge space and the stage is tiny, you might need to rehearse in a smaller area to see if your moves still work as well in a different context. If some moves just don't work on a small stage, again, you might have to adapt. The opposite is also true: if you're used to rehearse in a tiny space and end up on a big stage, your routine might seem a bit too small. If you've got space, try to use it as much as you can!

- How far is the audience from you?

This one is especially important if you've planned some audience participation, for example if you want to ask an audience member to pop a balloon in an area you can't reach, if you need an audience member for participation, etc. If you're performing your routine on a theatre or theatre-like venue, you might not be able to get close to the audience. In this case, if you absolutely need an audience member for your routine to work, you might have to ask a fellow burlesque performer to fill in.

On the other hand, if you're very close to the audience, be careful where you throw your clothes, especially anything heavy! You don't want to blind your first audience with a rhinestoned heel.

- What type of venue is it?

This one is a bit more subjective, but getting a feel of the venue is not a bad idea, especially once you have more routines to offer. If the venue is particularly classy, it might not be the best place to perform a super daring alternative routine (though you never know!).

Most importantly it might give you an idea of the type of audience to expect. If the promoter has a regular show in the venue, ask them directly: is the audience usually loud, quiet, rowdy, appreciative, full of "burlesque virgins" (UK burlesque jargon for people who have never been to a burlesque show), vintage enthusiasts...

It might be daunting to go onstage the first time and face a very quiet audience, but depending on the culture of the country you're in and the type of venue, a quiet audience can be a good thing. If you're performing in a country different from your own, check how people show their appreciation there. For example, in France, people whistle when they enjoy a show / performance, whereas it would be the opposite in the UK!

Don't worry too much though, burlesque audience are usually friendly and enthusiastic.

ON-STAGE!

Play with the audience

- Don't be scared to interact with your audience. Even if you don't interact directly, I don't necessarily mean audience participation here, but simply acknowledging you're on stage in front of people, who are looking at you doing your thing. Burlesque is different from acting in a play where you must pretend the audience doesn't exist, it's a live/living show. Unless your routine is more on the theatrical side, make eye contact, be playful, give teasing looks...

Don't be scared to improvise!

- Sure this might be easier once you have more experience, but playing with your audience and improvising is part of the fun! A couple of examples: the audience reacted loudly to you taking off your dress and is suddenly a bit quieter as you're undoing your corset. Give them your best "cheesecake" offended look and signal them to be louder. See how they react. Another one: pretend to take off an item, then give the audience a teasing look, indicating "no, no, no" with your finger.

These are just relatively common ideas, but depending on your routine, your personality, the audience, then you will find your own way.

In case of mishap...

- I mention that before but it's worth saying again. Costume mishaps happen. All. The. Time. They're part of the job! Don't fret and keep going. It doesn't mean your routine is ruined. Just don't panic, if you're stuck into something you can pretend to be teasing the audience until it comes undone. If it's really really stuck you might have to break out of something and fix it later. If an item of clothing comes off on its own too early, just pretend it was part of the routine all along. If your wig falls off, pull your best shocked face and put it back on in a funny way, or just let your hair down wildly as if it was always the plan. There's always a way to save it and if there isn't, it's not the end of the world, just move on to the next part of your routine.

- If you forget a move don't worry either. It happens, especially at the beginning if you're a bit stressed. Don't forget the audience doesn't know your routine, they won't realize if you forget a move, just keep dancing and nobody will notice you missed a step.

I think that just about covers it for our first show section... now there is only one thing left to discuss, how to take your burlesque career further.

Chapter 6: Developing your career

So your first show went well, you loved performing and the audience loved you. You might have already done a couple more shows as a "newbie", and you might be booked for a few extra shows. You're already working on your second and third routine. Time to upgrade and become a real professional!

Get pictures and videos!

This is so important if you want to get more bookings! I know many people don't like to see themselves on picture or on film. I even know of many burlesque dancers who love being onstage but absolutely hate seeing the video or the pictures. Yet it is absolutely essential to have some professional shots, live performance pictures, and videos of your routines to further your career.

On a side-note: if you've taken pictures or videos of the other performers, never release them online without asking for permission first. It seems obvious but it happens all the time. A lot of events have their own professional photographer, who will know how to get the best light and the best angle from performers. Random performance shots can be unflattering, especially if you're caught mid-pose or mid-move.

If there was a professional photographer at an event you performed at, do ask for the pictures! Sometimes they will be on the event's website or Facebook page, but the photographer might not release all the pictures of the event. On occasions, the photographer might not know all the performers and does not release the pictures without authorization.

Get pictures of your act

- A mix of on-stage pictures and photo-shoots is ideal for your burlesque performer CV. Try to get as many pictures from your act(s) as possible, if there is no official photographer for the event, enlist a friend to take pictures of you on stage at the beginning. It's best to only use professional pictures, but if you've only performed at one or two shows, it might not be possible. So get as many as you can to give promoters an idea of what your act looks onstage.

- Get some posed professional pictures taken in your costume(s). Depending on where you live, finding a photographer who does burlesque / pin-up / vintage etc. photography might be easy or not, so don't be scared to explain what you're looking for if the photographer has never worked with a burlesque dancer before.

- You might have to pay for a photo-shoot to get exactly what you want, or you might find a photographer who's interested in shooting a burlesque performer in their costume. Some photographers offer "TFP", time for print shoots. If you want something specific, it's unlikely you will find a photo-shoot where you get paid, but TFP is a good option to grow your portfolio.

Videos are essential

I know I mentioned videos before but it's vital you get some videos of your act if you're going to develop your career. You need videos of your act to get booked by organizers who've never seen you.

- If the venue and the promoter allow filming, always ask someone to film you. It doesn't have to be a professional film, a video from a mobile phone will work, just ask your friend or fellow performer to get a clear view of you.

- To further your career and develop your brand, you might consider filming a professional video of your act. Sometimes, venues or promoters will have a cameraman filming the show, but it's quite rare for small to medium events.

- It's a bit costly but if you're starting to develop your career, it might be worth investing in a few pro videos. You might need to book a space (rehearsing space, venue...) for a few hours and find a professional who can do it for you. It's worth it once you start applying for big events, especially if you only have low quality videos of your routines.

- Once you have a few good videos of various acts further down the line, it's a good idea to do a video resume, with an excerpt of each of your routines.

Burlesque Festivals

Burlesque festivals and contests over the world

Burlesque festivals represent a fantastic opportunity to develop your career. Festivals regroup burlesque performers from all over the world in one place, and will allow you to meet people you might have never got a chance to meet otherwise. It gives you a chance to see other fellow performers onstage, and to get a flavor of what's happening in other countries. It's also a fantastic chance to get your name out there, make contacts, and make yourself known internationally. If you win an award, you will also gain more exposure, you might be mentioned online and in various magazines, and you can mention it when you apply to other events.

There are lots of opportunities to perform in festivals and burlesque contests all over the world, but especially in the UK, US and Australia. I cannot mention them all here, but just so you're aware of a few famous ones, and can start attending or applying, here's a very quick, non exhaustive overview:

- UK: London Burlesque Festival organized by Chaz Royal since 2007, the biggest UK festival, happening every year around May https://www.londonburlesquefest.com/ and the Scotland International Burlesque Festival, organized by the same team, in June https://www.scotlandburlesquefest.com/

There are burlesque festivals and contests happening all over the UK: Burlesque Idol in Leicester, the North Wales Burlesque Festival, the Tassel Off in Leeds... if you live or travel in the UK, you're spoilt!!

- Western Europe: I already mentioned the UK as there is so much happening there burlesque-wise, but there are burlesque festivals all over Western Europe! Paris, Toulouse, Lyon, Berlin, Munich, Lisbon, Ibiza... I cannot list them all but just check what festivals exist in the country you're in.

- Eastern Europe: There's the Bohemian Burlesque Festival in Czech Republic in November https://www.bohemianburlesquefestival.com/about, the Prague Burlesque Festival in March http://www.pragueburlesquefestival.cz/, the Croatian Burlesque Festival in May http://cro-burlesque-festival.com/en/home/.

Eastern Europe as a whole however has rather few burlesque events compared to Western Europe. There was a Polish Burlesque Festival in 2015 but no follow-up.

- Australia: This Australian Burlesque Festival takes place in various cities: Sydney, Canberra, Melbourne and Hobart http://www.australianburlesquefest.com/ but there are many, many other burlesque events, festivals and contests taking place down under. Burlesque Idol. Miss Burlesque Australia http://missburlesqueaustralia.com/. There's even a burlesque museum.

- US: the US might be the place with the most burlesque shows, events, contests, festivals and venues in the world, so if you live there and you want a career in burlesque, you're definitely in the right place. Just to mention a few: Ohio Burlesque Festival, Texas Burlesque Festival, New Orleans Burlesque Festival... and of course the famous Miss Exotic World Contest at the Burlesque Hall of Fame.

Asia: Burlesque is popular in China and Japan, with many events taking place all over the countries. Burlesque is also now happening in Singapore, with Sukki Singapora's Singapore Burlesque Club.

These are just a few examples, and by no means an exhaustive list! New events and festivals pop up all the time, just keep your eyes open and follow burlesque blogs, pages, social media accounts. http://21stcenturyburlesque.com/ and http://www.burlexe.com/ are a couple of good websites to check out.

Market yourself!

It's not enough to know what is happening and where, if you want to develop your career, you need to learn how to market yourself.

Professional tools

- Build your website: if you can, get a professional website done, with a contact or booking option. You might not get lots of bookings through your website directly, but it's a great window and you can send the link to promoters when you apply to shows.

A few suggestions of section to add: About section with a description of your burlesque persona, videos, gallery with descriptions of your acts, list of previous performances and awards, contact page...

- Business cards: get cards made with your burlesque name, pictures and contact details to give away at events. Even if you don't get many direct bookings this way, people will remember you and it might open new opportunities.

- YouTube channel: Create a YouTube channel where you upload all your performances videos, and maybe a video resume. Again, you can give the link to promoters when you apply, and it will increase your visibility.

The legal bit

- Check whether someone else already uses your burlesque name, and check whether it is trademarked. Even if it's not trademarks but you find out someone else is using it, you might want to rethink your name. You want something that's original, and you don't want to be confused with another performer online. (Nor do you want a lawsuit.)

- Register to Equity in the UK, or similar if you live in another country: https://www.equity.org.uk/ They offer memberships with contracts you can print and use when you get booked for events.

- Register as self-employed in the country you live in: don't forget burlesque is a job. If you start getting paid for it, then you'll have to be registered as self-employed, and you'll have to pay taxes.

The next steps: A few ideas to further your brand

Teaching and putting on your own burlesque shows...

You've made it! You've become a successful full-time burlesque dancer. Now you might want to further your brand even more. The options are endless:

- you might start teaching other future burlesque dancers and create your own school

- you could go corporate and perform for companies

- you could start a hen do business

- you can start putting on your own shows

- you might make your own burlesque clothing brand!

The world is your oyster. Enjoy your burlesque career, and we will explore the many options to further your brand in the next How To book.

Conclusion and useful addresses

I hope you enjoyed this little How To book, and you now have a better idea of how to get your burlesque career started. It is by no means intended to be exhaustive, however it has some tips I wish I'd known when I first started. If you're not sure of what kind of performers you would like to be yet, don't worry. Developing as a performer takes time, and you're only just starting your journey.

Do not hesitate to go back to the beginning of the book and start again, research in more details burlesque performers of the Golden Era, watch as many videos of old-school and recent routines, educate yourself on the current star performers, check out blogs and websites but most importantly, find out where there are live shows playing in your area and go see burlesque. Support the scene and learn from seeing professional performers live.

Go back to the chapters describing classic routines and try them at home. See what works for you. Do your hair and make-up like you're getting onstage tonight. Rehearse and ask for feedback. Practice makes perfect.

Burlesque is a wonderful, colorful and crazy world, with a rich history which surface we've only scratched here. Performing onstage can be exhilarating, and if you enjoy it, it has the potential to be the best job in the world.

Focus on the basics, work on your routine(s), work on your costume(s), rehearse until you know your moves by heart and then go, put yourself out there.

Burlesque has been back with a vengeance since the late 90s, and it looks like it's there to stay. More shows, more events and more festivals are popping up everywhere everyday. You just have to dare going for it.

Useful addresses you might want to check out:

https://www.thelondoncorsetcompany.co.uk/

A large choice of corsets, from cheap beginners' corsets to more expensive steel-boned and waist training corsets.

https://www.corset-story.com/

Large choice, American based website.

http://thevioletvixen.com/

A favorite of mine for corsets, with a large and original selection

https://www.loveburlesque.com/corsets.html

Reasonable prices, not a huge selection but nice gothic style corsets.

- Many performers also sell tassels, costumes, headdresses... check out your favorite performers' social networks and websites and discover a treasure trove! Here are a few who sell their goodies online:

https://www.houseoftrixieblue.co.uk/trueblue

For embellished accessories, tassels, and custom requests.

http://www.daisycutterburlesque.co.uk/shop/456733 2474

For underwear and pasties. Also on Etsy with a larger selection.

http://www.talulahblue.com/costumes.html

For bespoke costumes and feather fans. Also on Etsy with vintage finds and gowns.

https://boudoirbydlish.bigcartel.com/

For the most glamorous gowns.

https://www.facebook.com/Archnia.Wigs/

For avant-garde custom wigs.

https://www.etsy.com/people/PassionflwrCreations?

Creator of amazing head pieces.

About the Expert

Emilie Declaron is a content writer and literary translator with over ten years of experience. She speaks five languages including English, French and Bulgarian, and currently works all over the world.

Emilie performed as a burlesque dancer in her twenties, mostly in the UK where she lived but also in continental Europe. She ran her own burlesque show from 2012 to 2015, the Lady Loco events in the North East of England, and also organized one-off variety events in various venues. She still is an avid supporter of the scene and follows closely any recent development in the burlesque world.

HowExpert publishes quick 'how to' guides on all topics from A to Z by everyday experts. Visit HowExpert.com to learn more.

Recommended Resources

- HowExpert.com – Quick 'How To' Guides on All Topics from A to Z by Everyday Experts.
- HowExpert.com/free – Free HowExpert Email Newsletter.
- HowExpert.com/books – HowExpert Books
- HowExpert.com/courses – HowExpert Courses
- HowExpert.com/clothing – HowExpert Clothing
- HowExpert.com/membership – HowExpert Membership Site
- HowExpert.com/affiliates – HowExpert Affiliate Program
- HowExpert.com/writers – Write About Your #1 Passion/Knowledge/Expertise & Become a HowExpert Author.
- HowExpert.com/resources – Additional HowExpert Recommended Resources
- YouTube.com/HowExpert – Subscribe to HowExpert YouTube.
- Instagram.com/HowExpert – Follow HowExpert on Instagram.
- Facebook.com/HowExpert – Follow HowExpert on Facebook.